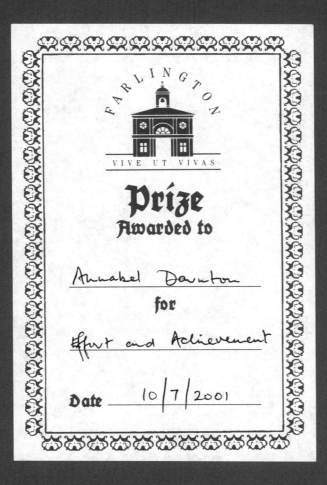

FARLINGTON

VIVE UT VIVAS

Prize
Awarded to

Annabel Dawnton

for

Effort and Achievement

Date   10/7/2001

THE VILLAGES OF
Hampshire

PAUL LIPSCOMBE & BARRY SHURLOCK

COUNTRYSIDE BOOKS

Other counties in colour portrait series include:

BUCKINGHAMSHIRE	LEICESTERSHIRE & RUTLAND
CHESHIRE	LINCOLNSHIRE
DERBYSHIRE	SUFFOLK
DEVON	SURREY
DORSET	SUSSEX
ESSEX	WARWICKSHIRE

Other counties in this series include:

HERTFORDSHIRE
SUFFOLK
SURREY

First published 1999
Photographs © Paul Lipscombe 1999
Text © Barry Shurlock 1999

All rights reserved
No reproduction permitted
without the prior permission
of the publisher:

COUNTRYSIDE BOOKS
3 CATHERINE ROAD
NEWBURY, BERKSHIRE

ISBN 1 85306 599 4

Designed by Mon Mohan
Produced through MRM Associates Ltd, Reading
Printed in Singapore

Contents

INTRODUCTION

Villages have an enduring appeal and are a great antidote to the complexities of modern life. Few counties have as many attractive places as Hampshire, where extensive conservation measures have retained much of the traditional fabric of the countryside. To take a short walk, lunch at the pub and wander round the ancient church of some village is still one of the great pleasures of life. Each place is unique, a happy mix of plan and accident, and yet each tends to have similar features. It is this simplicity and predictability which makes our villages so attractive.

Hampshire is an immensely diverse county, stretching from the coastline in the south to the soaring downs of the north, with the great slopes of the hangers to the east and the New Forest in its southwestern corner. Trying to define the 'typical' Hampshire village is a fruitless task. It contains villages of many kinds, some almost suburbs of nearby towns, others with a strong agricultural base, some on the fringes of forest, others on the banks of a chalk stream, some rarely visited and others on the tourist trail. Selecting those to photograph for this book has involved difficult choices, but the emphasis has been on villages of great charm, like Breamore, Mottisfont and the Meons, as well as those associated with famous sons and daughters, such as Selborne, East Wellow and Steventon.

By common consent, there are certain features of villages which score highly. Near the top of the list must be a good pub, with a friendly patron, a pleasant garden, good food and a fine range of ales. Thatched cottages are eternally attractive, partly because they are no longer built but also surely because they have a prettiness which modern builders cannot touch. A river brings much to a village, ideally with extensive water meadows and a bridge or two where the clear waters of the Hampshire chalk can be viewed en route to the Solent. Watercress, trout and ducks are also highly desirable parts of the Hampshire tableau, to be found throughout the valleys of the Test, Itchen, Meon and elsewhere. Village greens are highly prized, like those at Cheriton and Breamore, but with the exception of the New Forest, most areas of Hampshire have had their commons enclosed.

Perhaps a less obvious attraction of the village is the story it can tell. Many of the villages in this book have fascinating links with events which together make up the heritage of the county: Charles I at Titchfield, the planning of D-Day at Southwick, Hambledon and the birth of cricket, Cheriton and the Civil War, Laverstoke and the Bank of England, the Roman town of Silchester, and much else. It is a virtually endless list, with many famous names, some of which are mentioned in the following pages. Taking the time to get to know the villages of Hampshire is not only a great pleasure, but one which is forever full of surprises.

Barry Shurlock
Abbots Worthy, 1999

Bucklers Hard and the Beaulieu River

At Bucklers Hard you feel that you could build a boat, launch it and set off to any part of the world. In the 18th and 19th centuries the Royal Navy did just that, and in the 1960s the singlehanded round-the-world yachtsman Sir Francis Chichester set out from here. No doubt the monks of Beaulieu Abbey also made use of the river in their time. The place is a gift for seamen (*opposite*) and it is only surprising to find that it did not play a larger part in national maritime life. One who thought he saw the opportunities to rival the ports of Lymington and Southampton was the 2nd Duke of Montagu. In the 1720s he built a model village, with about two dozen cottages facing each other across an open green (*inset*). Unfortunately his plans foundered, but after 20 years the considerable settlement he had built at Bucklers Hard came to life as a shipyard.

The first naval ship to slip into the Beaulieu River was the *Mermaid*, a 24-gun warship built in 1745. In charge of the yard was Henry Adams, who lived in the Master Builder's House (now a hotel) and built a total of 43 ships for the Admiralty, which is a record for a private contractor. His family ran the yard for more than a century. The traditions of those men who built warships from trunks of New Forest oak can be glimpsed in the maritime museum. Tourism is yet another phase in the life of Bucklers Hard.

Today the maritime business of Bucklers Hard is carried on in Agamemnon Boatyard, which takes its name from the first ship commanded by Nelson.

During the Second World War the Beaulieu River was used for a variety of activities. Motor torpedo boats were repaired and serviced. Wooden minesweepers, which set off enemy mines with a towed magnetic device, were fitted out. An experimental floating dock and components for the artificial harbours used for the D-day invasion were also built here. And unknown to other users of the river, were the Special Operations Executive training men and women in the arts of subversive warfare and sabotage. In 1969 a plaque was unveiled in Beaulieu Abbey to the 'men and women of the European Resistance Movement who were secretly trained in Beaulieu to fight their lonely battle against Hitler's Germany'.

Keyhaven

Keyhaven is the only fishing village in Hampshire. It is also a sailing village and an ideal natural harbour (*inset*), sheltered by the huge mass of shingle which makes up Hurst Spit. The river is too tiny to have been of use to more than local vessels but this has preserved its character and makes it a pleasant place to visit after a day spent messing about in boats. Visitors are rewarded by outstanding sea views, with the high lands of the Isle of Wight in the distance, and the outline of Hurst Castle and its lighthouses.

Walking the length of Hurst Spit, which is about a mile and a half long, is like climbing a mountain on the flat.

The castle at the end was originally built by Henry VIII to protect Hurst Narrows, where the Isle of Wight is only a mile from the mainland. An unwilling visitor was Charles I, who was kept here for 19 days in 1648, following his imprisonment at Carisbrooke Castle on the island. In the 19th century it was massively extended as part of Palmerston's plans for strengthening the defences of the Solent. Together with a telegraph station and Hurst's two lighthouses, there was once quite a community on the spit.

During the summer a ferry plies between Hurst and Keyhaven, where life centres on the quay, the sailing club, the boatyard and The Gun Inn. Nearby is Hawker's Cottage, the 'little gunning place' of Colonel Peter Hawker (1786–1853), who came here to shoot wildfowl. Hawker's published *Diary* shows that in more than half a century's wildfowling he killed 29 species of birds. His total bag of Brent Geese alone numbered 1,327.

Between Keyhaven and Lymington stretch the marshes of a county council nature reserve, where people now come armed with binoculars. It supports a huge population of many species of sea birds which feed on the salt marshes. A sea wall (recently renewed) stretches all the way to Lymington, for this, with Keyhaven, is an area long under threat of flooding. Hurst Spit, which is breached from time to time, is the primary 'breakwater' and requires constant efforts to keep it intact from westerly storms.

Boldre

Men of the cloth in the New Forest were once more like missionaries than country clergymen. Their parishioners were scattered over a wide area and included gipsies and beggars, not much inclined to the scriptures. Boldre (pronounced *bolder*) was once the mother church of the southern half of the forest, with parochial powers over Sway, East Boldre, Brockenhurst, and also Lymington, which only gained its freedom in 1869. Even today, the parish extends over a large area of the west side of the Lymington River.

Boldre church (*opposite*) is wonderfully situated on high land, where huge oaks grow. The village is to the south, where the Fleur de Lys pub shares custom with the Red Lion. The churchyard contains the tomb of the Reverend William Gilpin (1724–1804), a celebrated writer and painter, a one-time headmaster who obtained the living of Boldre from a former pupil. He was one of the first to encourage an appreciation of the countryside as 'beautiful', rather than merely frightening or boring. He toured the Lake District and Scotland, and wrote and illustrated influential essays on landscape for the painter and tourist. Although lacking mountains, the New Forest had much to enthral him, especially the view from the windows of the rectory at Vicars Hill, Boldre. His tomb is beneath a large ash tree to the south of the church.

Despite its isolated location, Boldre has often been close to conflict. Threats of piracy, French invasions and war were never far away. Nearby Walhampton House was long the home of the Burrard family, including several admirals, who worshipped in the church and are buried here. It is therefore perhaps no surprise to find that the church contains a memorial to HMS *Hood*, which was sunk by the German battleship *Bismarck* in 1941. What is surprising is that this is the only monument for a catastrophe which cost the lives of 1,417 officers and men. Apparently 'when it became clear that no official memorial was to be raised,' the widow of Vice Admiral Lancelot E. Holland, who went down with the ship, decided to do something locally. Only a few years before the war, her husband had donated the inner doors of the south porch in memory of their son.

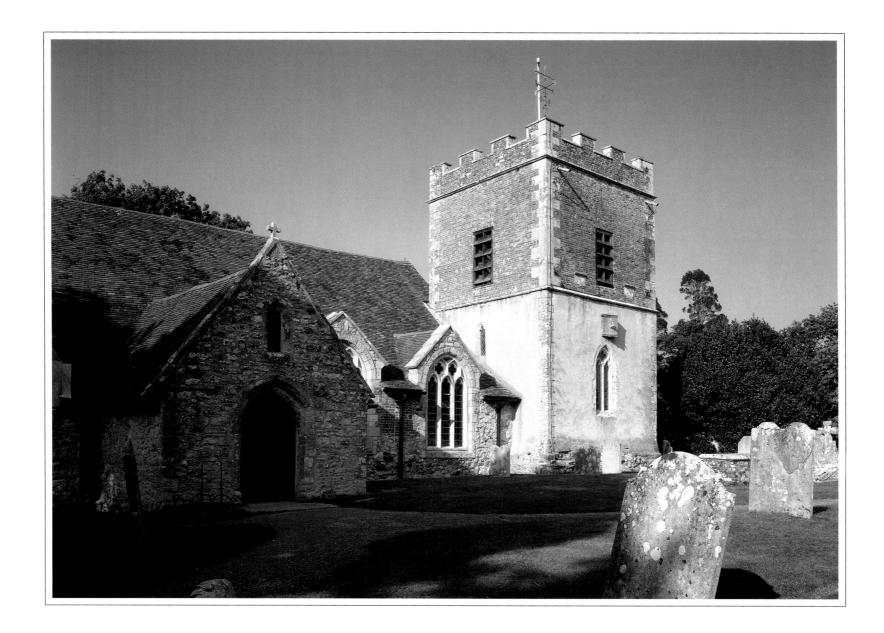

Minstead and Fritham

It is easy to forget that the 'traditional' patchwork of fields of southern England is the result of enclosing over centuries what was once the open countryside. Wandering through the great expanses of the New Forest today is a welcome breath of fresh air, yet even this was a form of enclosure, created as a royal hunting reserve by William the Conqueror in 1079. Settlements and villages in the New Forest are few and scattered, the poor quality of the land lending itself to afforestation rather than farming.

Minstead lies in the northern part of the forest, just to the east of the A31 road. It is a neat little village where you can find a cream tea or a pint of beer. Its pub, The Trusty Servant, (*opposite*), is named after a fictitious creature created at Winchester College, part pig, part ass, part stag. A panel outside the pub displays this curious beast, together with the school's famous motto *Manners Makyth Man*.

Sir Arthur Conan Doyle, creator of Sherlock Holmes, is buried at Minstead, together with his wife, in a grave near a large oak tree on the south side of the churchyard. He lived at Bignell Wood in the north of the parish (but died elsewhere). Nearby is the site where William Rufus, son of William the Conqueror, was murdered (or accidentally killed?) while out hunting in 1100. The body of the king was taken to Winchester via Romsey Abbey by a local man, John Purkiss.

A couple of miles west of the Rufus Stone lies Fritham, (*inset*), a charming hamlet at the end of a narrow lane. It belongs to Bramshaw, a parish once divided between Wiltshire and Hampshire. Eyeworth Pond, which lies half a mile beyond The Royal Oak pub at Fritham, is also called Iron Wells, but seems to have been created in about 1870 for a gunpowder factory, which used charcoal made nearby.

Ellingham and Ibsley

According to the Royal Observatory, the sundial above the south porch of Ellingham church (*opposite*) is 5 minutes 35 seconds slow. Leaving astronomical calculation aside, this magnificent wonderfully maintained timepiece must be one of the finest in the country. Today, this part of Ellingham is tucked away in a cul-de-sac near the busy road between Ringwood and Salisbury. Nearby, machines make gravel mountains and create pleasant lakes.

Ellingham became embroiled in national affairs in the late summer of 1685, when James II put down the Duke of Monmouth's unsuccessful rebellion. In the aftermath, two of the Duke's supporters found shelter at Moyles Court, the home of an elderly widow, Alice Lisle. Her late husband had been amongst those who had signed the warrant for the execution of Charles I during the Civil War. Now, when it was discovered she had harboured traitors, she was put on trial at Winchester and sentenced by the notorious Judge Jeffreys to be burned at the stake. The sentence was afterwards changed to beheading, but nothing could save the old lady. The chest tomb of Alice Lisle still stands in Ellingham church, to the right of the south porch. A headstone found in the tomb (probably belonging to another member of the family) contains the chilling words:

Life is a Vapour,
Death outs Life,
The Vapour disappears.

Moyles Court, just inside the New Forest, is now a boarding school.

To the north of Ellingham lies Ibsley, where The Old Beams Inn provides a pleasant place to 'refuel' and a stone bridge nearby somewhere to stand and stare. The waters of the Avon (*inset*) are prized by fishermen, not only for trout and salmon, but also for those prime coarse fish, the barbel, bream and roach. Across the meadows can be seen the lofty tower of Harbridge church, rebuilt by the Earl of Normanton about 150 years ago. The family seat, Somerley Park, lies to the south, on the opposite side of the river from Ellingham.

Rockbourne

The fertile valley of the Hampshire Avon marks the edge of the New Forest. Rockbourne lies two to three miles to the west of the river. It is situated in the Martin peninsula, a tongue of land which reaches out from Fordingbridge and includes a point, near Woodyates, where Dorset, Wiltshire and Hampshire meet. These are long-settled agricultural lands, with deepcut ancient lanes, which continue unchecked to Salisbury. Much is downland, once grazed by huge flocks of sheep. Rockbourne is a long thin village, with the Rose and Thistle pub at its centre and a fascinating complex of medieval buildings around Manor Farm, including a 13th-

century chapel and an Elizabethan range. The village takes its name from the seasonal stream, or winterbourne, which runs down the west side of its pretty street (*inset*).

Today, most people come to Rockbourne to see its Roman villa. It was discovered in 1942 when a farmer on the West Park Estate noticed fragments of tiles and oyster shells. During a trial excavation, local antiquarian A. T. Morley Hewitt discovered a mosaic floor. He bought the land and after nearly 20 years of excavation, had uncovered one of the largest Roman villas in the country. It had more than 50 rooms, some with hypocausts for underfloor heating, and two bathing suites. The full extent of the mosaics, which are covered in winter to prevent frost damage, also came to light.

Close to this site stands an imposing monument of 1827 to Lt-General Sir Eyre Coote (1726–83), who was born in Ireland but came to settle in Rockbourne, where he bought the West Park Estate. A brilliant tactician, his career as a soldier is best known for the defeat of the French in Madras in 1760, ending their hopes of dominating India. He and his family have other monuments in the church (*opposite*). In the 19th century the village was co-owned by members of the Coote family and the Earls of Shaftesbury. The 1st Earl, Anthony Ashley Cooper (1621–83), was the eldest son of John Cooper of Rockbourne and became a famous statesman, surviving (not unscathed) the twists of fate delivered by Cromwell and the subsequent restoration of Charles II.

Breamore and Wood Green

There can be few places of such contrast as the villages of Breamore and Wood Green, which lie together on the eastern edge of the flood plain of the Hampshire Avon. Breamore is an ancient settlement with a Saxon church 1,000 years old, whilst Wood Green is a pioneer development carved from the New Forest in the late 1600s.

In fact, much of the fabric of Breamore village also dates from the 17th century and many of its lovely thatched cottages were owned by the local estate until the 1950s. People come to see the Saxon rood in the church (*opposite*) and to visit Breamore House, an E-plan Elizabethan house which is interesting in its own right and now incorporates a countryside museum and much else. Local people, who grazed sheep, cattle and geese on Breamore Marsh, regularly trudged up Wally Hill to the House to pay their rent. They called it 'going to Wally Hill Fair'. A mile to the northwest is the mysterious Mizmaze, which contains eleven concentric rings. It was recut in 1783 but is of unknown origin. The garden of the house contains a modern maze involving 1,200 ft of brick path. Its design, based on a five-bar gate, won the Great British Maze competition in 1983, organised by *The Sunday Times*.

The people of Wood Green subsisted on the surrounding commons; the droves they cut to enable them to drive animals to and fro still survive. The village even now has the character of a frontier settlement, recognised by its designation as a conservation area. The aim is to protect the overall 'feel' created by those smallholders who built homesteads (and hovels) on unclaimed forest land and eked out a living in this remote corner of Hampshire. There is a simple church, built in red brick as a church room in 1914, a shop and post office and the Horse and Groom pub.

For those with an interest in art, Wood Green also contains a remarkable surprise, namely, a set of murals painted in the 1930s by two students from the Royal College of Art. These decorate the walls of the village hall and depict local life at the time.

Titchfield

Titchfield is one of those places which has managed to stay still. A century ago it might have been thought a small town; today it is a large village (*opposite*). Its centre has the dignity of a town and thankfully has been skirted by main routes. It stands on the estuary of the River Meon, a small chalk stream which rises near East Meon in the south of the county. Nearby are smallholdings which grow delicious strawberries.

A pleasant way to approach Titchfield is via the footpath which runs along the canal from the Solent shore, where Titchfield Haven is now preserved as an important nature reserve. It was once a significant inlet, which enabled shallow draught vessels to reach the village centre. All that was changed by the 1st Earl of Southampton in the early 17th century when he blocked

the mouth of the inlet in order to try to reclaim the marshland and build a 'New River'. The scheme cut Titchfield's seaward link and signalled the end of the port. Local anger expressed itself in the burning of an effigy of the Earl each year, probably the origin of Titchfield's present day carnival, now held around November 5th. Today, a few small yachts moor behind a shingle bank in a tiny harbour, with access limited by tides.

The existence of a navigable waterway probably led to the foundation in the Saxon period of an important minster church at Titchfield. Substantial traces of Saxon stonework can still be seen. Its influence eventually stretched from the Hamble River to Portsmouth Harbour, but was progressively chipped away by development and urbanisation. After the dissolution of Titchfield's 13th-century abbey the site and its buildings were acquired by Thomas Wriothesley, Earl of Southampton. His fine mansion, Palace or Place House, was itself largely demolished in 1781. His grandson was a patron of William Shakespeare and tradition has it that the first performance of *Romeo and Juliet* took place in the superb tithe barn which still stands nearby. The Earls of Southampton are commemorated in the village church, (*inset*) which stands next to the river.

Place House is open to the public and well worth a visit. It was here that Charles I came after his flight from London in 1647, thinking that he would find sanctuary in Carisbrooke Castle on the Isle of Wight. Instead he was betrayed, imprisoned, and eventually taken back to London en route to the executioner.

Portchester Village

Portchester village lies at the tip of a peninsula at the head of Portsmouth Harbour, overshadowed but not overwhelmed by a modern conurbation. Its tiny green, the Cormorant pub and a pleasing mix of houses are typical of many villages, but its unique feature is the castle, originally built in the 3rd century by the Romans and still in a remarkably good state. Portchester has long been a focus for visitors and little has changed over the years. People still come to see the castle, to climb to the top of the medieval keep, and to look out over the harbour, with breathtaking views of Spithead and the Isle of Wight.

It is said that Portchester Castle is the most complete fort of its kind in Europe. The walls are more than 1,700 years old, run for half a mile, include 14 bastions and are 18 ft high and 10 ft thick! The Normans recognised its strategic importance and built a castle within a castle. It also contains a medieval priory church (*opposite*), built by Augustinian canons, who later moved to nearby Southwick. During the Napoleonic Wars large numbers of French prisoners were kept here. Many major projects, such as the building of turnpike roads, depended on their labours.

Today, Portchester still benefits from its proximity to the sea (*inset*). Pleasant hours can be passed watching the yachtsmen and the comings and goings at the sea lock at Port Solent, a modern marina on the opposite shore. During the Middle Ages Portchester was used frequently by royalty as a port of embarkation for the continent. It was also well placed for huntsmen. Substantial tracts of the great Forest of Bere which dominated the landscape to the north of Portsdown Hill, still survive, including West Walk Woods near Wickham. Today, the main features are the scars of chalk quarrying and the Victorian redbrick forts built by Palmerston to secure the safety of 'Fortress Portsmouth'.

Southwick

Beyond the densely built slopes of Portsdown Hill is a hinterland of extraordinary rural seclusion. Within it lies the village of Southwick (*opposite*), almost every acre of which is privately owned. It might have been otherwise, because Richard Norton, one of the former owners made a will, published in 1727, bequeathing all his estates to Parliament for the aid of the poor, sick and wounded. Unfortunately for them, the courts found his will invalid by reason of insanity!

The hand of the Thistlethwayte family and its Southwick Estates can be seen in the uniformly painted doors and windows of its properties (*inset*) and in the well-padded box pew in the church. It also owns the Golden Lion pub, behind which is preserved an early

19th-century brewhouse. The last brewer was George Olding, a man of some guile, who paid part of the wages of the man who did most of the hard work with 'all the beer he could drink'. The secrets of the brewing process for what were called 'Hunts Home-Brewed Ales' were kept hidden by banishing the workman from the brewhouse at crucial stages.

The mementoes on the walls of the Golden Lion indicate that Southwick was where, in a manner of speaking, the D-Day landings were hatched. The wonderful village hall was opened in 1994 to mark the 50th anniversary of the operation. The planning was carried out in nearby Southwick House, the former grand mansion of the estate. Here General Eisenhower and his staff masterminded the exercise which kept Hampshire and the South overstretched in the months leading up to June 1944. The operations board still hangs in the wardroom of the naval establishment which now occupies the house, namely, HMS *Dryad*, the RN School of Maritime Operations and Maritime Warfare Centre.

The village has its origins in the priory of Black Canons which was founded at Portchester in 1133 by Henry I, but later moved to Southwick. This explains the unusual dedication of the village church, which is called St James-Without-the-Priory-Gate. Virtually nothing remains of the priory itself, except for traces of the fish ponds used by the community. The place was well fed by the streams which eventually become the Wallington river and enabled the mansion to have a fine lake, which still exists to the south.

Langstone and North Hayling

One of the prettiest seaside spots in Hampshire is at Langstone, which was the port for Havant but has now been encompassed by Chichester Harbour. Here stands the Royal Oak pub and Langstone mill (*opposite*), once powered by wind and water. The mill was bought in 1932 by the well-known Petersfield artist Flora Twort. Amongst her many guests was the novelist Nevil Shute, who wrote *The Pied Piper* here. The ruined tower of Warblington Castle is a mile to the east and Hayling Island on the opposite shore. On a clear day, Chichester Cathedral can be seen more than eight miles away. The village was connected to Hayling Island by a wadeway, traces of which can still be seen at low water. The first road bridge was built in 1824 and then, 50 years later, came the bridge for the Puffing Billy railway.

Langstone once thrived on its maritime trade. Today, apart from the activities of the Langstone Sailing Club, the closest that most residents come to the sea is when it surges up the High Street on exceptional tides and strong winds. Then local people insert their flood boards and watch anxiously.

Hayling Island is marinas and farming in the north and holidaymakers in the south, where the monks of Jumièges from Normandy built a mother church in the 12th century. Unfortunately the church was swallowed up by the waves. Even earlier, the Romans had built a temple in the north of the island. It lay about a quarter of a mile to the south-west of St Peter's church, North Hayling,

which is itself of considerable interest. Its simplicity is one of its charms, the main church dating from c1140, with a single addition about 100 years later. Meanwhile, Norman masons had moved on from round pillars to square ones, a transition which is apparent in the half-round-half-square pillars at the east end. Equally intriguing are the main supports of the porch, which were cut from the same tree and are mirror images.

The churchyard of St Peter's (*inset*) contains the grave of Princess Yourievsky, a member of the Russian royal family who managed to escape from the Bolsheviks.

Rowlands Castle and Idsworth

Rowlands Castle and Idsworth are on the very edge of Hampshire, between what were the territories of the West Saxons and the South Saxons. Rowlands Castle takes its name from a medieval castle that was sliced through by the Portsmouth and London Direct Railway, which opened in January 1859. Traces of the fortress remain to the south of the village centre, but even before the railway its foundations had been extensively undermined by chalk quarrying. Prior to this, the place was an isolated outpost on the eastern fringes of the Forest of Bere. It was certainly well placed to receive smuggled booty from the quiet waters of Chichester and Langstone harbours. According to tradition, the eponymous Rowland was a giant or a free-booter, or both!

In 1748 the village hit the headlines when a customs man and a witness he was accompanying were murdered by the son of a local publican and other men. They had been involved in the smuggling of tea and had been seen at work on the coast by shoemaker Daniel Chater. News of his journey to testify before a Chichester magistrate reached the smugglers, who brutally silenced their victims. Subsequently, seven of them were hanged.

Rowlands Castle (*opposite* and *inset*) is a planned village, created largely by the Victorians, who built pleasant villas around a lozenge-shaped green. It never was a well-defined parish, falling within the areas served by three different churches, those of the Redhill district of Havant (which eventually became the parish church),

Warblington and Idsworth. Most of the village then fell within the district of Idsworth, its chapel of St Hubert standing in splendid isolation in open country two miles to the north of Rowlands Castle. This wonderful church was restored in 1912 and contains fine wall paintings of about 1330.

Rowlands Castle was an important area for mustering troops prior to D-Day. In the summer of 1944, the village green was used as a tank park. Before the troops left for the beaches of Normandy, King George VI paid a visit and bade them God speed. The event is marked by a memorial stone in Manor Lodge Road.

Hambledon

Hambledon was once a busy small town with a market hall, until better roads drained away its trade and left the sleepy village we see today. Its charming main street, the broad High Street leading up to the church and its delightful surrounding countryside give it the feel of a classic English village. The banner headline, 'People's Market', above the village shop is said to refer to a market granted by King John. Its parish extended to the tithings of Chidden-and-Glidden, Ervills and Denmead. Were it not for the presence of the Bat and Ball Inn and Broadhalfpenny Down, it would be hard to credit that the national game of cricket first came to prominence here in the second half of the 18th century (*inset*).

Hartridges, the soft drinks company, which has been in existence since 1882, sponsors the Hambledon Cricket Club. Its ground, however, is now down in the village and Broadhalfpenny Down is used by the Broadhalfpenny Brigands Cricket Club. They have just built a wonderful new cricket pavilion, with a perky clock tower, on the hill, beside the Bat and Ball Inn, where Richard Nyren was landlord and cricketing 'patriarch'. His cousin, John Nyren, described this 19th-century golden age in his classic *Cricketers of My Time*: 'There was high feasting held on Broad-Halfpenny during the solemnity of one of our grand matches … Half the county would be present, and all their hearts with us'.

Another heart-stirring time in the village was in May 1944, when just before D-Day, George VI inspected Allied troops in Chestnut Meadow, off the Denmead road and opposite Kings Rest, where Charles II had slept in 1651 after fleeing from the Battle of Worcester.

A pleasant path leads past Hambledon church (which contains traces of its Saxon origins), up to the edge of a vineyard. The well-kept lines of vines produce some fine vintages. Indeed, Hambledon wine has been produced since the early 1950s, when General Sir Guy Salisbury-Jones showed the world that decent wine could, after all, be produced in these latitudes.

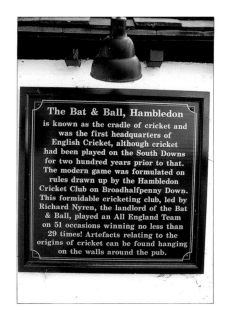

The Meons

The Meon valley is one of the prettiest parts of Hampshire, running between lofty downs and containing some of the most agreeable villages in the county. Three of them contain the name of the small but delightful river, called after the *Meonwara*, the Jutish Saxons who settled here (and on the Isle of Wight) in the 6th century. The road that runs along the west side of the Meon, today the A32, has since 1800 provided a route between Fareham and London, via Alton.

Meonstoke straddles the river, with its pub and church conveniently situated away from the main road and most of its cottages on the east side of the river. It was once owned by Winchester College and before that the bishops of Winchester, the major landlords in the valley. The connection is reflected in nearby Old Winchester Hill, now a major nature reserve. Tradition has it that this stunning place was once intended as the site of what became the city of Winchester. In reality, its earthworks show that it was a prehistoric settlement.

At West Meon the A32 leaves the valley for Alton, via the curiously named West Meon Hut, now little more than a pub. Thomas Lord, founder of Lord's Cricket Ground, lies buried at West Meon. His foresight in providing a home for the Marylebone Cricket Club did much to endear the national game to the capital. The Thomas Lord pub celebrates the man, who shares the churchyard with the spy Guy Burgess, whose remains were interred in the family grave in 1963.

East Meon (*opposite* and *inset*), with its tall-spired church beneath Park Hill, is the crowning glory of the valley, which is perhaps why it became the centre of an ancient hundred and manorial court, the stonebuilt courthouse of which still stands. The River Meon rises from a spring about a mile to the south of the village, to become the centrepiece of the main street (and in the past a frequent source of floods!), on its way to the sea at Titchfield Haven.

Selborne

From time to time the quiet village of Selborne has been shaken by shocking events. In 1484 it was the suppression of the priory. In 1830 it was the activities of the 'Selborne Mob', ill-fed agricultural labourers who terrorised the neighbourhood. Then in January 1990 a storm felled the 1,400 years old Great Yew, which had a girth of 26 ft and was probably planted soon after the missionary Birinus came to spread Christianity in these islands. It is well documented in the works of Gilbert White (1720–93), sometime curate of Selborne and widely recognised as the first English ecologist. It is impossible to visit Selborne without being reminded of the man, who in 1789 published his great classic, *The Natural History and Antiquities of Selborne*.

Selborne is a delightful village in its own right (*opposite*), situated in the hanger country of East Hampshire, where beech woodlands hang precipitously from steep slopes. It is an inspiring and distinctive landscape which erupts from the more gentle slopes of the county as if it were volcanic. Walking up the Zig-Zag, a path which Gilbert White and his brother cut above Selborne, is one way to appreciate this phenomenon. Another, less arduous, is to descend into Petersfield via Stonor Hill on the A272. The old butcher's shop (*inset*) is typical of many local buildings, which were constructed from a hard form of chalk called malmstone.

In 1954, The Wakes, where Gilbert White lived and died, was purchased to open a museum devoted to his life. This was made possible by a donation from Robert Oates, on condition that the museum should also include displays on the lives of two of his ancestors, both explorers, Frank Oates (1840–75) and the more famous Captain Lawrence Oates (1880–1912). The latter died on Scott's ill-fated expedition to the Antarctic and uttered that classic English understatement: 'I'm just going outside and may be some time.' Perhaps Gilbert White said the same thing to his housekeeper as he set off on another foray!

Cheriton and Tichborne

The River Itchen rises near Hinton Ampner House, before flowing north through Cheriton and Tichborne to join the Alre on the outskirts of Alresford, where it turns due west. This part of Hampshire has been civilised and settled for more than 1,000 years. Distantly sandwiched between the A272 and the A31, and protected by conservation laws, it seems likely to endure for some while.

Cheriton (*opposite*) is classically pretty, with the central green surrounded by cottages and threaded through by the river. How did such tiny places manage to achieve such charm? The answer, of course, is that they were bypassed by the pressures of urbanisation and 'discovered' by fugitives from the towns, who wanted to preserve what had been destroyed elsewhere. They are economic fossils, and all the better for being that! However, Cheriton has experienced horrific moments: it was almost wiped out by the Black Death, and on 29 March 1644 witnessed a battle as bloody as anything seen in recent times.

The Battle of Cheriton took place between Royalist and Parliamentarian armies on the high land to the east, near Cheriton Wood. It lasted six hours and involved 12,000 men, many hundreds of whom were killed or maimed. The entire village must have been traumatised by the event, which was 'won' by Sir William Waller for Parliament.

Tichborne has no great trauma to its past, although the existence in the church of a Catholic aisle marked off with iron railings signifies a religious upset not unrelated to the Civil War. This was the break of Henry VIII with Rome,

which meant that the Tichborne family, lords of the manor since the Conquest and staunch Catholics, were out of pace with national events. The railings are a statement that in the country it was often possible to compromise on the great issues of the day. Certainly the Tichbornes, seated at Tichborne House, managed to survive and to keep their hold on the village. The four stained glass windows in the nave (*inset*) are touching memorials to four nephews of Mrs Mary Egerton, her only four, all lost in the First World War.

Old and New Alresford

The necessity of making clear that a place is older than somewhere else that was itself founded in the early 13th century is one of those eccentricities which makes the English countryside so interesting. The 13th-century settlement is New Alresford (*opposite* and *inset*), a bishop's town set up according to a standard plan. Its older and less photogenic cousin is to the north, across the other side of a great dam built by a bishop of Winchester to create a huge pond for farming fish and powering mills.

Old Alresford proper with its triangular green lies below the church, which has its own settlement of several large properties. Foremost of these is Alresford House, built with an admiral's prize money. Sir George Brydges Rodney (1719–92) had been brought up at nearby Avington House, when his father's fortune disappeared in the South Sea Bubble. Rodney had a long, somewhat patchy career, culminating in 1782 in a brilliant action in the West Indies against the French fleet. His formidable character is perhaps best summed up by his words: 'I require obedience only. I don't want advice'. Rodney lies buried in a vault in the chancel of Old Alresford church, which also contains a splendid marble monument to his wife, Jane, who died at the age of 27 in childbirth.

It was in Old Alresford that Mary Sumner (1828–1921) started to hold those meetings of young mothers which became the Mothers' Union. She lived in Old Alresford Place (now a diocesan retreat) with her husband George, who was the rector. The activities of the Mothers' Union spread throughout the British Empire and provided a focus for dignifying the process of bringing up children and keeping house. It perhaps encompassed the roots of feminism before feminism had even been invented.

Subsequently George Sumner was appointed to a bishopric and his son, George Heywood (1853–1940), became a celebrated designer and architect.

Ovington, Lavington and Avington

Villages on the south bank of the River Itchen between Alresford and Winchester have retained the charm and character of isolated settlements. Ovington, Lavington and Avington share the Anglo-Saxon suffix 'ington', meaning 'meadow place', but that is their only similarity. Ovington has a pub and a church, and Avington is an estate village, which once belonged to the owners of Avington House. Lavington is hardly a settlement at all, no more than a fine Georgian house and a farm.

Ovington (*opposite*) is today best known for the Bush Inn, situated near the river and oozing with character. Long after the introduction of decimalisation, it still insisted on presenting its menu in pounds, shillings and pence! Nearby a footpath runs over a footbridge and along the Itchen river bank. This is a delightful rarity hereabouts, as most Itchen landowners have long kept the public from their banks.

The contrast between Ovington today and about 130 years ago, when it had a population of 163, is emphasised by a contemporary guidebook which shows that the place was then endowed with a shop, two shoemakers, a blacksmith, a post office, and a 'brewer and beerhouse'. All this was presided over by Baroness Elizabeth Von Zandt, of Ovington Park (now Ovington House).

The road between Ovington and Avington is narrow and winds beneath steep banks. The lands on the north side of the river are less precipitous, which may explain why the larger villages developed on this side. Avington (*inset*) is so much an estate village that the Georgian parish church, with its amazing box pews, stands in the park of the great house. Its home farm is a mile to the south, near Hampage Wood. By all accounts, the local people were treated generously by the owners of Avington House and rallied to protect local property from a mob from Winchester during the agricultural riots of the 1830s.

The mansion house is spectacularly sited overlooking an artificial lake – sadly, now drying up – and has a long history. Charles II stayed here with his mistress Nell Gwynne as guests of the notorious Countess of Shrewsbury. Its owners until 1848 were members of the Brydges family, dukes of Chandos. Today it can be contemplated from a pleasant picnic area beside the lake.

The Worthys

The Worthys, a string of attractive villages on the north bank of the River Itchen, originated from a great Saxon estate that spread from the walls of Winchester. Traces of this period exist in Headbourne Worthy church, well known for its Saxon stonework and its rood, a sculpture of Christ on the cross. The *Anglo-Saxon Chronicle* records that the royal court once assembled at Kings Worthy. An extensive Saxon cemetery has been discovered in the grounds of Worthy Park, and the remains of the houses of the people buried there were uncovered during the building of the M3 motorway in the early 1980s. Mill Lane, Abbots Worthy, must be one of the oldest named streets in the county, appearing as *Mylan Weges* in documents more than 1,000 years old.

The largest of these villages today is Kings Worthy, which started to mushroom in the Springvale area after the First World War. The old village lies on the route of the Silchester–Winchester Roman road, new evidence for which was found during the recent construction of church rooms. Amongst a pleasant collection of houses around the church is the Old Post Office (*inset*), which owes its origins to a Receiving House opened in 1845, one of the first post offices in the country.

When the original Saxon estate became divided into parishes Kings Worthy was administered with Barton Stacey, Abbots Worthy (owned by the Abbot of Hyde, Winchester) with Micheldever, whilst Martyr Worthy (*opposite*) became part of the Easton estate of the bishops of Winchester.

Like so many places in Hampshire, The Worthys played their part in the Second World War, notably on Worthy Down, where there was a military airfield. Worthy Park was commandeered by the military, and the A33 served as a huge parking lot for tanks prior to D-Day.

The Worthys have always provided a good living for farming folk, whilst the river, copses and downs provide ample opportunities for country sports. It is scarcely surprising, according to a local saying, that 'Worthy folk always come back to be buried.'

Stoke Charity and Hunton

The Dever passes through a string of pretty villages, all tiny with the exception of Sutton Scotney, which has been swollen by the influence of the Newbury road. The river provides sport for trout fishermen and nourishes water gardens and cress beds.

Stoke Charity is a crossing place that took its name from

a 13th-century lord of the manor, Henri de la Charité. Remarkably, the structure of the church, which stands in magnificent isolation (*opposite*), has scarcely changed since his day for, unlike so many other places, Stoke Charity has shrunk! In 1830 the journalist and traveller William Cobbett commented on the decline of the village, which he said had once had ten farms. Now, he said, everyone was 'half-starved except the curate'!

The church contains a very fine depiction of the Mass of St Gregory, a Catholic icon which was suppressed by decree in the Tudor period. There are many examples of such decrees being ignored, but it was a dangerous game so that the priest at Stoke Charity apparently decided to embed the lovely sculpture in the wall of the church. It lay undiscovered until 1849, when the church was restored. There is much of interest to see in the tiny building, which is crammed with tombs and memorial brasses.

The prehistoric people in this part of the Dever valley were protected by Norsebury Ring, the hillfort which stands to the north of Stoke Charity. A tiny lane leads from the village over the stream, turning left towards Hunton (*inset*) with a tiny church. Hard though it is to imagine, what is now the A34 road to Newbury once passed through the main (and only) street of Hunton.

Micheldever

Take a local guidebook from about 1850, or even earlier, and it could still serve as a useful companion to the village of Micheldever (*opposite*). What has changed most is at East Stratton across the A33, where the lords of Micheldever, the Barings of banking fame, lived in a great mansion in Stratton Park, which has long since been pulled down. Much of Micheldever is now owned by the Eagle Star Insurance Company.

The Baring touch is everywhere in Micheldever. In 1806, a few years after acquiring the village as part of the Stratton Estate, Sir Francis, the founder of Barings Bank, settled a bill for £10,000 for rebuilding the church after a devastating fire. The result was the airy, domed, octagonal nave which still stands. The baronet also commissioned the famous sculptor John Flaxman to make three family monuments for the church, which are widely regarded as some of his best work. The 2nd baronet, Sir Thomas, built almshouses, as well as the present school, with its wonderful clock tower, which cost a mere £160.

Micheldever included the tithings of Northbrook (later taken as a Baring family title), Southbrook, West Stratton (linked by a funeral path) and Weston Colley. It was endowed with some very productive holdings, such as Borough Farm, which is still the very picture of agricultural prosperity by the road to Stoke Charity. The estate also held Micheldever Wood, a mile-long swathe of trees, seen from the M3 which cuts through it.

One of the greatest blemishes to mark Micheldever was the hanging in 1830 of a local lad, Henry Cook. He had assaulted a magistrate, who happened to be a Baring, during disturbances which took place at the time of the agricultural riots. Many must have muttered: 'Serve him right', but his death, at the age of 19, emphasises the terror of the ruling classes at the time, who feared a re-run of the French Revolution.

Laverstoke and Freefolk

For nearly 300 years the upper reaches of the River Test were dominated by the activities of the Portal family, manufacturers of paper for banknotes. The last Portal only retired from the then family business in 1968. Throughout most of its time the firm manufactured paper exclusively for the Bank of England, after Henri Portal had secured the contract in 1724. Henri was descended from a distinguished Huguenot family. In 1712 he set up his works at Bere Mill, near Whitchurch and later he moved his business to Laverstoke Mill, where as many as 100 workers were employed. The business extended into Overton after the First World War and was the site for a 'shadow' banknote printing factory set up in the Second World War by the Bank of England.

In the 1960s, when it could claim to be the largest manufacturer of banknote paper in the world, Portals was supplying security paper to more than 100 governments in five continents. Fortunately, long before anyone had heard of environmental protection, the industry which settled in this essentially rural area was one dependent on clean water. Indeed, it is in the direction of water treatment and environmental engineering that the company has expanded.

As the Portals accumulated wealth they acquired its trappings, notably Laverstoke House, set in extensive parkland and completely rebuilt in 1800 on the site of an older house. They also built workers' houses, almshouses (*opposite*) and other facilities, as witnessed by numerous plaques and datestones. Perhaps the most interesting relic is the house of 1785 built opposite Laverstoke Mill for 'Ye Bank Officer', who stayed here when supervising the manufacture of the paper.

Bere Mill survives – a cream-painted, weather-boarded, 'chocolate-box' building standing at the end of a long drive. It is situated in the former parish of Freefolk, or Freefolk Manor as it was once called, to distinguish it from the Freefolk Priors tithing of nearby Whitchurch. The tiny white-painted chapel of Freefolk stands opposite Laverstoke church and can be reached over a bridge (*inset*) from the road or from Bere Mill, via a pleasant footpath across fields.

Steventon

'Church of St Nicholas, Steventon, Hampshire' declares the noticeboard outside the church, as if to reassure the visitor. Even today, Steventon feels remote, though only a few miles from Basingstoke and a mile or two from North Waltham in one direction and Overton in the other. In fact, the main part of the village has drifted away from the church and the manor house and lies to the north, where a few cottages are ranged about a tiny triangle of grass. Nearby the road to Deane passes through a tunnel under the London-Southampton railway line on its way to Micheldever Station (originally called Andover Road) (*inset*), which is three miles from the village of

Micheldever. This awkward position was forced upon the railway engineers when the landowners of Steventon refused to allow a station to be built in their village.

For those not familiar with Hampshire's past, Steventon has one great claim to fame. Even if the advertisement in the lobby of the church for the Jane Austen Society of North American escapes attention, a plaque of 1936 on the north wall gives the game away, for Steventon is the birthplace of the great English novelist. The church is full of memorials to the family, though to appreciate the detail it is necessary to know that Jane's brother Edward adopted the name Knight when he succeeded to the estates (at Steventon and elsewhere) of his relative Thomas Knight. The Knights held the manor between 1706 and 1855, when it was sold to the Duke of Wellington, and Jane's father George was the rector from 1761 to 1801, when her brother James was appointed to the living. The rectorship continued in the family until 1873, first in the hands of another brother, Henry, and then with Edward's son, William Knight, who served for 50 years.

The parsonage house where Jane was born in 1775 stood on the right-hand side of the long, narrow lane which runs up to the church. Nothing can now be seen, though it is said that a well still exists. It was replaced by the handsome house on the hill opposite, now called Steventon House (*opposite*), which was built by William Knight a few years after his induction to the rectorship.

Old Basing

It is difficult to believe that the village of Old Basing, sandwiched between the M3 and the London railway line and now mainly a dormitory for Basingstoke, was once Hampshire's most powerful symbol of political and social change, far more significant than its upstart neighbour. In October 1645, despite two years of repeated batterings by Parliamentarians, Basing House, a stronghold of Royal power and influence, was still more or less intact. At that time, the owner was John Paulet, 5th Marquis of Winchester. The household was managing to hang on with the aid of consignments of food brought from the King's camp at Oxford, and elsewhere. The Marquis kept up his own spirits by scratching with a diamond the motto *Aimez Loyaulté* on every pane of glass in the house. Unfortunately for him, while his guards neglected their duties and played at cards, Cromwell and his men attacked in force. The house was burnt to the ground.

The great mansion of Basing House had been built in the 16th century by Sir William Paulet, one of the executors of the will of Henry VIII and Lord High Treasurer of England to Edward VI, Mary and Elizabeth I. When Elizabeth and her court stayed at Old Basing in 1560, she humoured Sir William, then aged 85, by saying: 'By my troth, if my lord treasurer were but a young man, I could find it in my heart to have him for a husband before any man in England'.

Today, the site of Basing House (*opposite* and *inset*) is open to visitors interested in the siege and its place in the

great conflict. More than a century after the fall of Old Basing House, the great estate of Hackwood Park, originally a hawking park, was created two miles to the south by successive Dukes of Bolton, as the Paulets became. With a circumference said to cover eight miles, it was, and still is, one of the greatest estates in the country.

Sherborne St John

Two miles north of Basingstoke lies this attractively named village (*opposite*). The Wey Brook or 'Sher' is a tiny tributary of the River Loddon which gives Sherborne part of its name. The 'St John' element refers to the family who until 1550 were lords of the manor. The lovely little 12th-century church in this long, straggling village is said to have two bells taken from Basing by Oliver Cromwell's order, after he had destroyed Basing House in 1645. More apparent treasures can be found along the village street, with its many lovely cottages. A Wealden house is a rare find in Hampshire,

more usually to be seen in Kent or Sussex, while another cottage has walls of solid chalk.

The church and rectory and the charming post office (*inset*) are extremely picturesque, but most people come to Sherborne St John to see The Vyne, an historic house a mile to the northeast, in the direction of Bramley. This Tudor mansion was built in the early 16th century for courtier William Sandys. Originally, the ancestral home was a simple moated manor house. The new mansion, with its own chapel, was described by John Leland as 'one of the principal houses in goodly building in all Hamptonshire.' The Vyne is set in parklands which run down to a lake formed by damming the Wey Brook. Facing the lake is a great classical portico, added to the house in the 1650s, and one of the first examples of what became the *sine qua non* of country houses.

In 1653 the Vyne and its estate were sold to Chaloner Chute, an eminent London lawyer who served reluctantly as Speaker in Richard Cromwell's parliament. The Chute family continued to occupy the house until the 1950s, when it was bequeathed to the National Trust. Among its treasures are a superb 18th-century staircase and a long oak gallery. The Tudor chapel has fine wood panelling, carved stalls and stained glass, depicting Henry VIII, his sister Margaret and his first wife Catherine.

Upton Grey and Weston Patrick

The pond at Upton Grey (*opposite*) is beloved of picture editors and has appeared in countless magazines and newspapers. It was where the postman blew his horn to summon people to collect their mail, and where the lamplighter tended a light hung on Pond House, the local tailor's home and workshop. When the pond froze over, candles in jam jars were arranged around the edge by children who came to skate. The buildings edging the long hill between Upton Grey church and the pond are a delightful 'accident' of architectural style and decoration. Perhaps this was why the village was chosen by Charles Home, founder and editor of *The Studio*, who came to live here in the early 1900s. He restored the original manor house by the church and modernised and extended Upton Grey House.

Faced in the 1920s with the need to build a village hall the ambitious idea of founding the Upton Grey and District Operatic Society was conceived. Performances of Gilbert and Sullivan were a sellout and before long the village had its hall.

Alongside Upton Grey lies the hamlet of Weston Patrick. Architect Thomas Henry Wyatt came to live hereabouts in the middle of the 19th century. He had designed the Adelphi Theatre and other public buildings, and now turned his attentions to Weston Patrick. First he rebuilt the parsonage house and then in 1868 the church, with its pretty bell-turret and miniature spire.

Weston Patrick suffered a terrible calamity in 1886, when a fire in one of its thatched cottages spread to eleven others and a house. When the Basingstoke fire brigade eventually arrived the village was a smoking ruin and 47 people were homeless. In any event, there was no water for the fire engine. Although the village was thereby denied its olde worlde charm, its cottagers no doubt slept more soundly under their tile roofs. The adjoining hamlet of Weston Corbett is a sizeable place which inexplicably almost died. In 1801 its population stood at a mere 10 souls; a century later it had climbed to 11!

Silchester

There are many parts of the world where deserted towns are commonplace, but they are rare in England. Silchester, which lies about seven miles north of Basingstoke, is one of the largest deserted urban sites in the country. It was the tribal capital of the Atrebates, who had fled from northern France to escape the invading Romans. They founded *Calleva Atrebatum*, an octagonally shaped settlement which eventually came to be a fully Romanised town with flint-and-stone walls 10 ft thick, 20 to 25 ft high and 1fi miles long. There are substantial remains of these walls (*inset*), notably near the parish church and beside Wall Lane.

The town was extremely well positioned, with roads to Winchester, London, Dorchester-on-Thames and Bath. There was a grand forum, a basilica, public baths and at least six temples. All this and much more is known from extensive excavations carried out by archaeological pioneers in the 19th century and up to the present day. A particularly noteworthy find was a tiny Christian church, the foundations of which lie beneath the turf about 300 metres west of the parish church. It is the earliest known Christian site in any town north of the Alps. The existing church of St Mary the Virgin, which contains many Roman bricks in its structure, can therefore justly claim to represent a tradition of Christian worship spanning 1,600 years (*opposite*). Near the church, opposite Manor Farm House, are the remains of the town's amphitheatre, where public meetings and perhaps gladiatorial contests were held.

Silchester fell victim to Saxon invaders at the end of the 5th century. Its existence was never forgotten by local people, who frequently unearthed relics, including beads, swords, tools and a Roman eagle in steel. Folklore attributed the town to a fabled giant called Onion and 'Onion's pennies' was the name given to the Roman coins which were occasionally found by farmers. In the 19th century, an enterprising Aldermaston publican set up a collection of Roman antiquities, but it is in Reading Museum that the full story of the town is laid out. There is also an excellent small museum on the site, housed in a green corrugated shed.

Ecchinswell and Sydmonton

The Hampshire Highlands, as this part of the county has been called, were already well known to walkers and country-lovers long before Richard Adams wrote his best-seller, *Watership Down*, published in 1972, which takes its name from that part of the escarpment between Ladle Hill and White Hill (*opposite*). This breathtakingly beautiful country is now favoured by the wealthy (and hang-glider enthusiasts), but in the recent past was dominated by the Earls of Carnarvon at nearby Highclere Castle. Here it was, Richard Adams wrote, that the light 'lay like a golden rind over the turf' and 'the insects buzzed, whined, hummed, stridulated and droned.' Here it was that Hazel and his companions came after fleeing from their warren and undertaking an epic voyage through deep woodlands in Ecchinswell.

Watership Down looks over the Sydmonton estate, with its fine mansion and old church, now deconsecrated, in private grounds. Those wanting a closer look at this delightful place can take a public footpath, which passes through the grounds. A large part of Sydmonton once belonged to Romsey Abbey. After the dissolution it was granted to John Kingsmill, whose descendants held it until modern times. St Lawrence's church in Ecchinswell contains a plaque commemorating local inhabitant Lionel Portman (1873–1940), singer and writer.

Ecchinswell (*inset*) was once the home of the Digweed family, who subsequently moved to Steventon, where the church contains a harrowing white marble monument to Mary Jane Digweed. In 1824 she died at the tender age of 16 in Brussels 'to the inexpressible grief of her parents.'

Faccombe and Linkenholt

These two tiny villages were once at the limits of habitation in this sparsely populated part of Hampshire. Today, their isolation is a virtue, making them ideal for shoots and other country pursuits; they are at their most hectic when leather sounds on willow (*inset*, at Linkenholt). But in the past they struggled to survive. St Barnabas church at Faccombe (*opposite*) dates only from the 1870s, when it took the place of the deserted church at nearby Netherton. The Victorian building contains some fine 16th-century memorials taken from the old church. Netherton has now been restored to glory and contains a wonderful barn thatched in traditional Hampshire longstraw, sporting the kind of 'straw fringe' that once gave charm to many old cottages. Faccombe is so isolated and so well looked after that visiting it has the feel of trespassing in someone's parkland. This is hardly surprising, because Faccombe is essentially an estate village. Without Faccombe Estates there would be no Faccombe. Even the pub, the Jack Russell, which serves superb fare opposite the village pond, is owned by the estate.

Linkenholt is even smaller than Faccombe. Covering about 1,000 acres, and never occupied by more than a few families (albeit large ones in the past), it has the character of an overgrown farmyard. The post office is an extraordinary survival in this outpost of rural living – and long may it continue. Within the last two or three generations, the population of Linkenholt has halved. The small church and the even smaller school alongside were built in architecturally matching styles, even down to the shepherds' crowns (fossilised sea-urchins) which decorate their window heads. They both date from about 1871. The school, now used as an estate office, was originally built to house 40 pupils and continued until 1938.

Despite the diminutive size of the village, life at Linkenholt manor house spared no luxury. Built in 1907 with 42 rooms, it was extended in 1935 to contain … a ballroom! Amongst the mod cons in the grand mansion was an early form of double glazing, presumably installed to economise on heating rather than eliminate noise.

St Mary Bourne and Ibthorpe

St Mary Bourne is in the valley of the Bourne rivulet, which runs from its source above Hurstbourne Tarrant (where it is sometimes called the Swift) into the Test at Hurstbourne Priors. As its name suggests, it is a winterbourne, which rises in February, traditionally on St Mary's Day and dries up in the summer.

The Bourne Revels were an annual summer event held in the small square before the George Inn (*inset*). A century ago entertainments might include two young men trying to beat each other senseless with heavy sticks, with the aim of being the first to draw blood. At least one contestant sustained brain damage and spent his last years in the county asylum. These activities must have earned the disapproval of the local surgeon, Dr Joseph Stevens, who is buried in the churchyard. He was not only a physician, but also studied the local antiquities, publishing his substantial *Parochial History of St Mary Bourne* in 1888. After leaving the village he became the honorary curator of Reading Museum.

The churchyard snugly abuts Gable Cottage like a piece of well-turned joinery. This is a proper churchyard, with a huge hollow gnarled yew tree – of unknown date, but clearly very much older than its neighbour, another yew planted in 1759. There is a wonderful collection of chest tombs of the Longman family, nearly all identical, the oldest 1708. One of the treasures of the church – and an eternal mystery – is the Tournai font. This is carved in a characteristic, black Belgian marble and was probably brought over by Henry de Blois, bishop of Winchester and grandson of William the Conqueror. There are eight of them in the country, including one at East Meon and another in Winchester, and this is the largest. But why here?

Above Hurstbourne Tarrant lies the hamlet of Ibthorpe (*opposite*), where many of the cottages are reached via tiny bridges over the Bourne. Here in this delightful spot stands Ibthorpe House, which was frequently visited from Steventon by Jane Austen. It was the home of her friends Mary and Martha Lloyd, both of whom married into the Austen family.

Knights Enham and Enham Alamein

The mother of this pair of villages, Knights Enham, is tucked away in a rural oasis, yet is within walking distance of Andover town centre. Despite the enormous changes that the area has seen, Knights Enham could be straight out of a Jane Austen novel.

Its humble 12th-century church (*inset*) is situated in the midst of farm buildings. The entrance to the church is tiny and low and some of its windows would not be out of place in a cottage. It has a small, oak-shingled tower and there are glimpses of stonework beneath rendering. Alongside stands the cream-coloured Regency rectory, now a private house. A large cemetery abuts open fields by the village street in the yard of Manor Farm. The influence of Knights Enham was once quite extensive and stretched to Doles Wood, three miles to the north, where the naturalist and writer George Dewar (1862–1934) roamed.

Other parts of the parish included East Anton (called 'Eastontown' on some gravestones), Upper Enham and Enham Alamein, which stands on the busy road to Newbury and takes its present name from the famous Battle of El Alamein fought in Egypt during the Second World War under Field-Marshal Montgomery. After the First World War a 'village centre' for disabled servicemen had been set up at Enham Place and a gift of money from the Egyptian government enabled this to be extended and developed to provide a setting for industries which could provide work for the disabled. The church of St George in the village acts as a focus for veterans who fought beside Montgomery. Nearby stands a fine, white-painted medieval house (*opposite*), which serves as an estate office and village museum.

The Clatfords

The Clatfords, on the west side of the river Anton, have always thrived because of the river. Consequently they are long and thin, following the flow of the water, with no obvious centres. The waterways themselves have been engineered with weirs and sluices to serve the mills that were so important. The prehistoric peoples of this area relied for protection on Bury Hill, the imposing hillfort which looks over the Anna Valley, where the Pilhill Brook enters the Anton just below the Andover ring road.

The name of the Crook and Shears pub in Upper Clatford (*opposite*) indicates the importance of sheep in the area. In fact, the name Clatford literally means 'the ford where the burdock grows', the burdock, or teasle, being used for combing sheep's wool. Agriculture of a different kind brought Wiltshire born Robert Tasker (1785–1873), to the Pilhill Brook to build improved ploughs and other machinery. Taskers were one of the companies to benefit from the repeal of the 'Red Flag' Act and went on to build many steam-driven tractors and traction engines. Although there is no heavy industry in the Clatfords today, many small businesses are run within its flint walls and thatched cottages. The late 12th-century All Saints church, Upper Clatford (*inset*) faces a small lake stocked with enormous goldfish. In 1954 its benefice was united with Goodworth Clatford and in 1977 they were joined with Abbots Ann. Both the Clatford churches have recently acquired elegant church rooms, attached directly to the old churches. That at St Peter's, Goodworth Clatford, is like a large gazebo.

Goodworth Clatford has a long association with the Iremonger family. Virtually all the stained glass in the church is dedicated to them, whilst three Iremongers served as rectors between 1782 and 1928, with only a nine-year period without a member of the family in office. The link continues in the churchyard, where the last interment of an Iremonger took place in 1997. For a village with such a long history, the Royal Oak at Goodworth Clatford is surprisingly recent: its predecessor was demolished during the Second World War, together with much else in the village, by what is said to have been the most westerly flying bomb.

The Wallops

The Wallops form a long thread of thatch and greenery which has retained its rural seclusion by being on the road to nowhere. Even the main route between them manages to avoid most of Nether Wallop and runs only to the small village of Broughton, where the namesake Wallop Brook falls into the Test. Over Wallop sports one of the oldest petrol pumps (*inset*) in the country. The one note of modernity is at Middle Wallop, where a military airfield has long been established. It is also the home of the Museum of Army Flying, from kites and balloons to eurofighters.

Middle Wallop is a sort of invented settlement and was the name given to the untidy bits and pieces which did not belong to Over (or Upper) Wallop and Nether (or Lower) Wallop. These relatively large villages have long had important country estates. That at Over Wallop is associated with the Lords of Portsmouth, whose family name is Wallop, whilst Nether Wallop is linked with the Lords Bolton, whose family name is Paulet.

Nether Wallop (*opposite*) is a labyrinthine village connected by narrow lanes. The Five Bells pub is easily missed! It is a village which has an irrefutable air of seclusion, a quality which probably helped to preserve the rare wall paintings in its late Saxon church. Maintenance was not a strong point of the churchwardens and oak splints erected to shore up collapsing pillars in 1752 were not removed, to make way for definitive repairs, until 1978. It was then that the wall paintings were discovered – those above the chancel arch dating from about AD 960 and attributable to the Winchester School, and *Christ and the Sabbath Breakers*, a much later painting made to strike terror into local hearts.

Nether Wallop church is also remarkable for other reasons. Since the 12th century its living has been in the hands of York Minster. And it must be one of the first churches to extend its reach to the internet (www.hants.org.uk/wallop/). What next?

Houghton and Mottisfont

Houghton (said *Hoe-tun*) runs along the west bank of the River Test from the outskirts of Stockbridge to Bossington Mill, a fine three-storeyed building. The Roman road between Winchester and Old Sarum – forerunner to Salisbury – crossed the river at Bossington and was particularly important as a route for bringing lead from the Mendips. The silt of the river has revealed at least one Roman lead ingot

Long and straggly, Houghton (*inset*) is divided into North Houghton and Houghton Drayton. North Houghton was the home of John Pain in the 19th century, who was one of the most celebrated shepherds or 'flockmasters' in Hampshire. The jewel of the village

is Houghton Lodge, a gentleman's residence in the cottage orné style, built in about 1800 beside the river.

The Natural Trust property Mottisfont Abbey (*opposite*) is delightfully situated close by the river, no doubt to take advantage of the copious spring, which still runs. It also benefited from a steady stream of pilgrims between Winchester and Salisbury, a hospitality perhaps echoed by its charming tearooms. The interior of Mottisfont Abbey is well known for the work of the theatrical artist Rex Whistler. His *trompe-l'oeil* work (literally, tricks the eye) makes you want to touch it, especially 'the smoking urn'. The gardens of the house contain a fine collection of historic roses.

An Augustinian priory was endowed at Mottisfont in 1201 by prominent landowner William de Briwere. It possessed mills, orchards, a tannery, dove houses, and all the other requirements of a prosperous self-sufficient community. After dissolution it passed to the Lord Chamberlain, William Lord Sandys of The Vyne, Sherborne St John. He built onto the priory church, but what can be seen today – still grafted onto the old church – is a mid 18th-century house, built by Sir Richard Mill.

Like Nether Wallop, the church at Mottisfont had links with York. This dates back to the 7th century, when Wilfrid, Bishop of York, was for a time exiled to the south of England. He founded Mottisfont church, outside the orbit of the Bishop of Winchester, and subsequently it became attached to the see of York when Wilfrid returned north.

East Wellow

At one time, nursing was regarded as degrading and nurses depicted as undesirables. It took the Crimean War and a national heroine to change attitudes. The popularity of Florence Nightingale, who came from the peaceful little village of East Wellow, near Romsey, reached almost hysterical proportions after reports of her caring for wounded soldiers in the Crimea. 'The lady of the lamp' might have quietly retired to East Wellow, but instead in 1861 she used the £50,000 raised in her honour by public subscription to found a nurses' training school at St Thomas's Hospital, London. It was the first of its kind in the world and influenced the training of nurses everywhere.

Florence Nightingale is buried at East Wellow, beneath a shining white pyramidal monument in the churchyard. This was erected by her as a memorial to her parents and only the initials 'FN', as she requested, show that she too lies here. Her father William Nightingale came from Derbyshire, to settle at Embley Park, now a boarding school. Even today this corner of Hampshire, on the edge of the New Forest, is relatively remote.

East Wellow church, which is entered via a pretty revolving gate (*inset*), is dedicated to St Margaret of Antioch, the patron saint of women in childbirth. Wall paintings (*opposite*) depict the saint in a famous scene in her life, when she resisted the advances of the local governor Olybrius. Until a few years ago the church also contained the Scutari Cross, made from musket balls given to Florence Nightingale during the Crimean War, but in 1991 this unique memento was stolen.

Kings Somborne

Kings Somborne is a relatively large village which lies between Romsey and Stockbridge, on the line of the old Roman road between Winchester and Old Sarum, which crossed the River Test at Horsebridge. The village (*opposite*) stands in an isolated position on the east side of the Test Valley, separated from the boggy lands of the river by a hill which was once John of Gaunt's deer park. The fence or 'park pale' can be traced for most of its circuit and is particularly noticeable by the Horsebridge road. Somborne – as it is often called – is watered by a

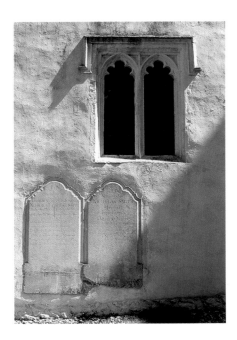

winterbourne, which flows beside the main street and in places has to be crossed by a ford.

'Chair seating' is the art of weaving those cane chair seats which look like a cross between a tennis racket and fine embroidery and it continues to be practised in King Somborne by Derek Oxley. People here have been making a living from wood crafts since the area was heavily forested. Regular coppicing of hazel, leaving only the 'stool' to regrow, was a technique which provided the raw material for a wide variety of woodland products. If you are looking for a sheep hurdle or fencing, Barker & Geary of Kings Somborne will oblige. Plenty of wood for fuel also made the place suitable for metal processing and in the 19th century three iron foundries flourished here.

The village has several satellite hamlets, such as Ashley (*inset*), yet is still far enough away from any sizeable town to retain a strong flavour of other-worldliness. It is no doubt still sympathetic to 'characters', though worlds away from the 1930s, when the bar of the Crown Inn was often propped up by Mossie, a man who made a living from selling mosses and leaf sprays. He had a marked dress sense and wore a green jacket, knickerbockers, grey stockings, a red-and-white neck-tie, and a pheasant feather in his hat.

In the 19th century Kings Somborne had an elementary school which became the pride of the nation. Founded as a National School in 1842 by the vicar, Richard Dawes, it was regarded as a model of its kind and drew a host of visitors, including Prime Minister Lord John Russell and the headmaster and writer Matthew Arnold.

Stockbridge

The layout of Stockbridge reflects its two staples of trade and trout. The main road between Winchester and Salisbury is crossed at right angles by the River Test (*opposite*), a chalk stream known to fishermen worldwide. Few places of the relatively small size of Stockbridge can boast so many fascinating shops, including those catering for the country sportsman and the art connoisseur. Filling up with petrol at the charmingly antiquated garage is no ordinary experience, whilst taking a drink at the Grosvenor Hotel (*inset*) is like dropping into a gentlemen's club.

Part of Stockbridge's success is surely that it is very contained – hardly larger now than when in about 1200 it became 'the street of Kings Somborne' at a spot where the Romans had built a causeway across marshy land.

To the west is the great earthwork of Danebury Hillfort, from which the ruins of the former grandstand of the racecourse, once of national repute, can be seen. At its peak the district had nine racing stables and drew enormous crowds in the summer months. Sportsmen of a quieter turn cast artificial flies onto the waters of the Test. The Houghton Club, once the leading fishing club in the world, was witness at Stockbridge to the development of dry-fly techniques. People here have always known how to make the most of country living!